Faithfulness, Gentleness, Self-Control

Fruit of the Spirit

Lane Burgland

Contributions by Robert C. Baker

CONCORDIA PUBLISHING HOUSE · SAINT LOUIS

Copyright © 2006 Concordia Publishing House
3558 S. Jefferson Ave., St. Louis, MO 63118-3968
1-800-325-3040 • www.cph.org

Written by Lane Burgland

Edited by Robert C. Baker

Prayers on pages 11, 18, 24, 29, 36, and 41 are from *The Lord Will Answer: A Daily Prayer Catechism*, compiled and edited by Edward Engelbrecht, copyright © 2004 Concordia Publishing House.

Unless otherwise indicated, Scripture quotations are from The Holy Bible, English Standard Version ®, copyright © 2001 by Crossway Bibles, a division of Good News Publishers. Used by permission. All rights reserved.

Scripture quotations marked NIV are from the HOLY BIBLE, NEW INTERNATIONAL VERSION®. NIV®. Copyright © 1973, 1978, 1984 by International Bible Society. Used by permission of Zondervan Publishing House. All rights reserved.

This publication may be available in braille, in large print, or on cassette tape for the visually impaired. Please allow 8 to 12 weeks for delivery. Write to the Library for the Blind, 7550 Watson Rd., St. Louis, MO 63119-4409; call toll-free 1-888-215-2455; or visit the Web site: www.blindmission.org.

Manufactured in the United States of America

1 2 3 4 5 6 7 8 9 10   15 14 13 12 11 10 09 08 07 06

Contents

About This Series

By this My Father is glorified,
that you bear much fruit and so prove to be My disciples.

Jesus, *John 15:8*

Only hours before Jesus was arrested, He delivered an important message to His disciples (John 14–16). At the heart of this message He describes the "fruit" His disciples would bear, the works they would do to glorify the heavenly Father. Through the gift of the Spirit, Jesus promised love (John 14:21), joy (15:11), and peace (14:27) to them and to you.

However, many Christian families and congregations do not exhibit the fruit Jesus (and later Paul) described. Selfishness, pride, and abusive behavior arise all too easily for us. Sin is truly second nature to human beings, even to the people of God.

This Bible study series will help you produce the fruit God calls you to bear as a believer. Through biblical examples and teaching from both the Old and New Testaments, you will explore God's goodness and blessings for you in Christ. You will learn to crucify "the flesh with its passions and desires" and to "live by the Spirit" (Galatians 5:24–25).

Student Introduction

Good living begins with good understanding. For this reason Jesus spent considerable time teaching His disciples before sending them out in service. Among the things Jesus taught His disciples was "every healthy tree bears good fruit" (Matthew 7:17). In other words, God's people will naturally want to do His will by doing good works.

Unfortunately, Jesus' illustration about good trees bearing good fruit has been used as a reason to ignore Christian education about good works. The argument has been made that since Christians will naturally bear fruit and do good works there's no point preaching or teaching about them. There's no point in studying them. Just let nature take its course.

Certainly you and all God's people need to have confidence that God's Word and teaching will lead to good works. But no congregation can ignore the truth that the sinful nature is still very much at work within the people of God (Romans 7:15–19). You need constant pruning! Jesus also taught, "Abide in Me, and I in you. As the branch cannot bear fruit by itself, unless it abides in the vine, neither can you, unless you abide in Me" (John 15:4). He called you to cling to both the Law of His teaching (which commands good works) and the Gospel (which causes good works to grow).

The Work of the Spirit

When the apostle Paul wrote to the Christians in Galatia about the "fruit of the Spirit" (Galatians 5:22), he wrote to a congregation afflicted with sin. The Galatians had eagerly embraced the Gospel. But soon after the apostle left to preach elsewhere, the Galatians divided into factions and were carried away by false doctrine. They erred in the most basic ways by confusing God's Law and Gospel (3:2–3), attacking one another (5:15), and growing conceited (5:26; 6:3). They had lost the patience, kindness, and goodness first cultivated by the apostle's preaching. In response, Paul writes to them not only about correct doctrine (chaps. 1–4) but also about Christian behavior: the fruit of the Spirit (chaps. 5–6).

The list of the "fruit of the Spirit" in Galatians 5 is not the only list of good works recorded in the apostle Paul's letters. (See 2 Corinthians 6:6; Ephesians 4:2; Colossians 3:12; 1 Timothy 6:11; and 2 Timothy 2:22 for other examples.) Yet it is Paul's most complete list and is especially directed to congregational members rather than church leaders. In this list of nine "fruit," the apostle summarizes what Christ wants to cultivate in you by His Spirit.

You did not choose Me, but I chose you and appointed you that you should go and bear fruit and that your fruit should abide, so that whatever you ask the Father in My name, He may give it to you. These things I command you, so that you will love one another.

John 15:16–17

To prepare for "Promised Faithfulness," read Genesis 12.

1

Promised Faithfulness

....and thereto I plight thee my troth.

The Form of Solemnization of Matrimony, *The Book of Common Prayer*

In wedding ceremonies where the traditional "King James" English was used, both bride and groom made a vow to each other. Modern couples, however, would be hard pressed to explain what "plight thee my troth" means. Updated versions of the vow seem clearer: "pledge you my faithfulness." The person promises to remain faithful to his or her spouse, forsaking all others and forming a lasting, loving relationship exclusively with that one special person they marry.

Throughout the course of their life together, each couple finds out whether they can keep that vow or not. Will temptation lure one of them into adultery? Will financial pressures break them up? Can they endure a lingering illness, the death of a child, the interference of an in-law, the stress of relocation? We don't know the quality and depth of a relationship until it is tested. Can we count on another person even when temptation or trial appears? Paul lists "faithfulness" as one of the fruits of the Spirit in Galatians 5:22. To better understand what he has in mind, we turn to God's Word. Can we count on God? Can God count on us?

Abraham, a Study of God's Faithfulness

God makes many promises in the Scriptures. In Genesis 12, we read about a promise he made to Abram, a man who lived about two thousand years before the birth of Jesus. Throughout the story of Abraham (his name was changed by God in Genesis 17:5), two strands intertwine—God's faithfulness and Abraham's faith.

Read Genesis 12:1–5 and answer the following:

1. Did Abram know his destination when God called him to leave the comfort and security of home?

2. Identify the seven parts of the promise God made to Abram.

3. How old was Abram when God made this promise? How many children did Abram have?

Read Genesis 15:1–6 for answers to these questions.
4. What problem does Abram raise?

5. How does God answer?

6. What proof did God offer Abram?

7. How did Abram respond to God's promise? Why?

Read Genesis 17:1–8.
8. Why did God give Abram a new name?

9. What additional promise did God make to Abraham (v. 8)?

Read Genesis 17:9–18.
10. What purpose did circumcision serve?

11. How will the faithfulness of Abraham's descendants impact the promise of land in later years?

12. How old was Abraham at the time of Isaac's birth?

13. How long did Abraham wait for God to keep His promise?

Joshua, Faithful toward God

Near the end of his life, Joshua gave a farewell address to the people he led into the Promised Land many years earlier. He summoned representatives from the twelve tribes that made up God's people at the time and reminded them of God's faithfulness. He also challenged them to remain faithful to Him. Read Joshua 23:14–16 and discuss the following:
14. How faithful was God to His promises?

15. What warning did Joshua make in this passage?

16. What is the heart of the covenant between God and His people?

In Joshua 24:1–13, this leader of God's people summarizes the history of God's faithfulness from the time of Abraham to the present. God called Abraham from paganism to faith, from a foreign land to Canaan (Palestine). God watched over the Hebrews during their sojourn in Egypt and rescued them in the exodus. He destroyed the pursuing Egyptian army and gave victory to the Israelites in their wilderness battles. God brought them across the Jordan River and delivered the Promised Land into their hands. Read Joshua 24:14–24.

17. What challenge did Joshua lay before the people?

18. What bold declaration of faith did Joshua make?

19. What surprising warning did he give the people when they said they also wanted to serve the Lord?

20. How did Joshua's last command (v. 23) reveal the peoples' unfaithfulness?

The Messiah, Faithfulness Incarnate

The prophet Isaiah, inspired by the Holy Spirit, looked forward to God sending a Savior who would bear the sins of all people. In Isaiah 11:1–5, he describes the coming Messiah.

21. List the seven characteristics of the Spirit that rests upon the coming Savior (v. 2).

22. List the three characteristics of the Messiah (vv. 3–5).

23. How will the Messiah demonstrate His faithfulness? How does His faithfulness impact you?

Blessed Lord, who has commanded us to love one another, grant us grace. Having received Your undeserved bounty, may we love everyone in You and for You. We implore Your mercy for all; but especially for the friends whom Your love has given to us. Love them, O Fountain of love, and make them to love You with all their heart, that they may will, and speak, and do those things only which are pleasing to You. Amen.

Anselm of Canterbury, 1033–1109

Sing "Let Us Ever Walk with Jesus" (*LW* 381; *TLH* 409).

Words to Remember

Now therefore fear the LORD and serve Him in sincerity and faithfulness. Joshua 24:14a

To prepare for "Enduring Faithfulness," read 2 Corinthians 1.

2

Enduring Faithfulness

God will send out His steadfast love and His faithfulness!

King David, *Psalm 57:3*

Faithfulness is a relational term. It implies a relationship existing outside of itself. In the case of *faithfulness*, the word refers to the quality of dependability and trustworthiness of someone to a particular standard or person. In a marriage, a partner is "faithful" to a spouse by forsaking all others. A person would be "faithful" to an employer by doing the job assigned to the best of his or her ability. A soldier is "faithful" to his country and his comrades by serving with honor (for example, the motto of the United States Marine Corps is *semper fidelis*, "always faithful"). As with the other fruits of the Spirit, we find faithfulness in God Himself.

God's Faithfulness

God keeps His promises. As we have seen in the Old Testament, God's children can depend on our heavenly Father's ongoing love, constant grace, enduring mercy, ever-present forgiveness, and help in time of need. He does not change His mind about us nor do His emotions shift and waver like ours do. In this part of the study we will look at three passages in Paul's letters to the Corinthians to see what God's faithfulness means to Paul.

Read 2 Corinthians 1:18–22.

24. Where do we find God's "Yes"? Why is it "Yes" and not "Maybe"?

25. Can we be certain of God's love? Why?

26. How are we able to stand firm in the faith through all the troubles of life?

27. What "deposit" has God given us as a seal of his faithfulness?

Read 1 Corinthians 1:4–9.
28. To what do the Corinthians owe their many spiritual gifts?

29. Will God keep us faithful to the end (see also 1 Thessalonians 5:23–24)?

Warning and Promise

Read 1 Corinthians 10:1–13.
We might be tempted to think that because we have been baptized, celebrate the Lord's Supper, and enjoy fellowship with Jesus Christ, that it doesn't make any difference how we live. We could take God's love for granted and turn forgiveness into a "license to sin." In this section, Paul offers both a warning and a promise.
30. What warning does Paul share (v. 12)?

31. What promise does he offer (v. 13)?

32. On what grounds does Paul base this promise?

Faithfulness under Pressure

Hard times and troubles test the strength of faithfulness in any relationship. In the history of the Christian Church, persecution has flared up and put tremendous pressure on believers. In the face of ridicule, torture, and death, God gives us the strength to remain faithful to Jesus.

Read Revelation 2:8–11.

33. What must the Christians in Smyrna soon face?

34. How do you measure faithfulness?

35. What promise does God make to His faithful people?

Read Revelation 2:12–17.

36. Who is the prime mover behind all persecution of Christians?

37. What did Antipas do and what price did he pay?

Read Revelation 13:1–10.

In Revelation 13, John introduces us to two beasts that serve the great dragon, Satan. The first beast (the beast from the sea) represents anti-Christian government and the second beast (the beast from the earth) symbolizes anti-Christian religions, especially those in service to a tyrannical government.

38. What should Christians expect when they live under an anti-Christian government?

39. What two qualities do the saints need in these circumstances?

40. To whom must the saints remain faithful as they endure persecution (see also Revelation 14:12)?

Read 3 John.

The Christian who continues to confess Jesus as Savior and Lord even under persecution demonstrates genuine faithfulness. Faithfulness also includes support of the Gospel in every way possible, as John shows us in 3 John. Read 3 John 1–8 and answer these questions:

41. To whom does John write this short letter?

42. What does John mean by "the truth" in verses 3–4?

43. What is Gaius doing for the "brothers" (traveling Christian missionaries) that John considers "faithful" (v. 5)?

Christ the Ideal

In Hebrews 3, the author compares and contrasts Christ and Moses. The writer of this epistle hopes to encourage his Jewish Christian readers to continue in the Christian faith even in the face of persecution. A return to Judaism would save them in the here and now from the physical and economic sufferings that lay ahead, but it would doom them to an eternity of suffering, separated from God. Part of the author's strategy in this section (3:1–4:13) stresses the superiority of Jesus over Moses. Read Hebrews 3:1–6 and answer the following:

44. Were Jesus and Moses both faithful to God?

45. What did Moses do that kept him out of the Promised Land?

46. Who or what is God's house?

47. How is the faithfulness of Jesus greater than that of Moses?

The author of Hebrews tells us that Jesus faithfully served God as His Son in mission and ministry, culminating in His sacrifice for us on the cross. Jesus' faithfulness also plays a critical role in another way. Read Hebrews 10:19–25.

48. How are we supposed to approach God?

49. How can we have a clear conscience before God?

50. We hope for eternal life through Jesus Christ. Why can we hold onto this hope without doubt or fear that God will change his mind?

51. Why should we continue to meet together (go to church)? What benefits does God give us there?

O God, by Your great love for this world, You did reconcile earth to heaven through Your only-begotten Son. Grant that we who, by the darkness of our sins, are turned aside from brotherly love, may—by Your light shed forth in our souls—be filled with Your own sweetness, embrace our friends in You, and our enemies for Your sake, in a bond of mutual affection. Amen.

Mozarabic Liturgy (c. seventh century)

Sing "Great Is Thy Faithfulness" (*HS98* 899) or "What a Friend We Have in Jesus" (*LW* 516; *TLH* 457).

Words to Remember

For the word of the LORD is upright, and all His work is done in faithfulness. Psalm 33:4

To prepare for "Gentleness in Service," read Isaiah 40.

3

Gentleness in Service

Nice guys finish last.

Common saying

As we look around at the world in which we live, we might think that nice guys—nice people—do indeed finish last. Football, basketball, baseball, and all other sports reward "aggressive" behavior: strength combined with the will to dominate and win. There seems to be no room for gentleness in sports. Likewise, in business, those who succeed and rise to the top of their field work hard, compete fiercely, and move past their rivals. It's a "dog eat dog" kind of world.

God works very differently from the way the world works. He deals with sinners gently, sending rain to the just and the unjust (Matthew 5:45). That means God provides generously and graciously for the physical needs of all people, even unbelievers. Even when God disciplines His children, He does not destroy us as our sins deserve. He tempers His discipline with gentleness because He loves us so richly and powerfully in Jesus Christ. As we will see in this session, our Savior perfectly embodies this gentleness as He shepherds His flock for salvation. Our Good Shepherd provides the ideal picture of gentleness, a genuine "fruit of the Holy Spirit" (Galatians 5:22).

The Old Testament does not describe God as "gentle" or as possessing "gentleness." Perhaps the reason for this lies in the Hebrew language, the original language for almost all of the Old Testament. It doesn't have a vocabulary word that means exactly "gentle." For example, take a look at 2 Samuel 22:36 in several translations. The KJV (the ESV is similar) translates: "thy *gentleness* hath made me great." The NIV offers: "you *stoop down* to make me great." The Hebrew original often means "to be afflicted, bowed down, or humbled" and God is never afflicted, bowed down, or humbled. He never finds himself in such situations. In 2 Samuel 22, David praises God for deliverance from his enemies and in verse 36 gives God glory for saving him and for condescending to help him

19

("you stoop down to make me great"). In other words, David does not praise God for being gentle, but glorifies Him for taking the time and trouble to help him, insignificant as he is.

The Old Testament does, however, often describe the coming Messiah as "gentle." The Messiah, faithful servant of the Lord, will fulfill His mission precisely by being afflicted, bowed down, and humbled. We find this most clearly prophesied in Isaiah.

Isaiah's Words of Comfort

The prophet Isaiah lived in the eighth century BC and brought God's word of judgment against Israel (the northern ten tribes) and Judah (the southern two tribes). God used Assyria to destroy Israel by the end of the eighth century BC. A little over one hundred years later, God used Babylon to lead Judah into captivity. Isaiah foresaw this captivity and knew that God would return a remnant of His people to the Promised Land. From that remnant would come the Messiah, God's anointed Shepherd. Looking ahead to the end of the Babylonian captivity, Isaiah brings words of comfort to God's battered and bruised people. Read Isaiah 40:1–5 and answer the following:

52. Isaiah comforts the people with the promise that their sins are paid for (v. 2). How does God accomplish this?

53. Who fulfills the prophecy of verses 3–4?

54. How will the messenger of verses 3–4 prepare the way for the Messiah's coming?

55. In what way will the glory of the Lord be revealed when the Messiah comes?

Read Isaiah 40:6–11.

56. Which is more powerful and enduring, the empires of humanity or the Word of God? Why?

57. Isaiah identifies two prime characteristics of the Messiah's advent in verses 10–11. What are they?

58. How does verse 11 speak words of comfort to you personally?

The Lord's Servant

Read Isaiah 42:1–4.

Isaiah introduces us to the Servant of the Lord in these verses.

59. What kind of relationship does the Lord have with His Servant in verse 1?

60. How does Isaiah describe the Servant's ministry in verses 2–4?

The following passage is the longest and most explicit of the "Servant Songs" in Isaiah. The prophet presents a powerful picture of the coming Messiah who endures affliction, humiliation, and even death for the sake of God's people.

Read Isaiah 52:13–15.

61. What promise does God make to His Servant at the outset (v. 13)?

62. What causes the disfigurement in verse 14 (see Isaiah 50:6)?

Read Isaiah 53:1–5.
63. What will the Servant of the Lord look like?

64. To what event do verses 4–5 specifically refer (see Deuteronomy 21:23)?

65. How does the Servant bring us peace?

Read Isaiah 53:6–9.
66. Is it a compliment or an insult to be compared to a sheep?

67. How does the Servant embody perfect gentleness in these verses?

68. The Servant obeyed God's law perfectly. Why then did He suffer the law-breaker's punishment?

69. Where would the Servant be buried?

Read Isaiah 53:10–13.

70. How do things turn out for the Servant of the Lord?

71. What does God give us as a result of His Servant's suffering?

The Messiah King

God called the prophet Zechariah to encourage the people to finish building the temple following the Babylonian exile. In Zechariah 9:9–13, he looks forward to the coming of the Messiah, God's anointed King.

72. Why should the people rejoice?

73. Normally a king arrived with great fanfare and grandeur. How will this King come to His people? Why?

74. What will this King accomplish? How are we members of His Kingdom?

God, You have taught us to keep all Your heavenly command-ments by loving You and our neighbor. Grant us the spirit of peace and grace, that we may be both devoted to You with our whole heart, and united to each other with a pure will; through Jesus Christ our Lord. Amen.

Leonine Sacramentary (c. fifth century)

Sing "I Am Jesus' Little Lamb," (*LW* 517; *TLH* 648).

Words to Remember

My sheep hear my voice, and I know them, and they follow Me. I give them eternal life, and they will never perish, and no one will snatch them out of my hand. John 10:27–28

To prepare for "Approaching Gentleness," read 1 Peter 3.

4

Approaching Gentleness

Blessed are the meek.

Jesus, *Matthew 5:5*

When we hear the word *meek*, we may well think of weakness and timidity. We might imagine a person who cannot stand up and deal with the problems in life or someone who has low self-esteem or is just plain shy. This is definitely not what Jesus has in mind. *Meekness* and *gentleness* describe an attitude of humility and self-restraint. The gentle man might be very powerful, physically strong, or socially empowered, but he interacts with others out of love and compassion.

Peter's Advice

In 1 Peter 3:1–6, Peter offers a case study in gentleness as an exercise of love and Christian concern. Imagine a situation where a Christian wife is married to an unbelieving husband. How shall she win him over to Jesus?

75. What non-verbal witness can a wife make to her husband?

76. What does the world define as "beauty"?

77. What does God see as beautiful?

78. Does what Peter says in these verses sound offensive to modern ears?

Paul's Exhortation

God calls all Christians, not only believing wives, to demonstrate gentleness in our interaction with each other. Read the following passages from Paul's letters.

Read Galatians 6:1–5.

79. How should we help someone who is caught in a sin?

80. In what way can we carry each other's burdens?

81. Is there any room for a "holier than thou" attitude in the Christian community?

82. What law of Christ do we fulfill when we deal gently with erring brothers and sisters?

Read Ephesians 4:1–6.

83. What calling have we Christians received?

84. What does the "unity of the Spirit" have to do with dealing gently with each other (contrast 1 Corinthians 3:1–3)?

85. What is the "bond of peace" (v. 3)?

Read Colossians 3:12–14.
86. How are we supposed to get along with people that irritate us and do things we don't like?

87. What binds us together?

The Yoke of Jesus

By nature we think that we must earn God's love. We work hard to get good grades in school and even harder to get raises and promotions at work. Surely God works the same way, doesn't He? The Bible teachers of Jesus' day talked about taking the "yoke" of the Law on their shoulders when they undertook to keep all of God's commandments in the Hebrew Scriptures. There are at least 623 of them and only the very devoted and committed could even try to keep them. Jesus offers a tremendous contrast. His way is simple, His "yoke" is easy—believe in Him. Read Matthew 11:25–30.
88. What has the Father revealed to little children that He has hidden from the wise and learned (see Matthew 19:13–15)?

89. What is the one way to the Father (see also John 14:6)?

90. How can Jesus give us rest?

91. Why is His "yoke" easy and His burden light?

92. How are His gentleness and humility revealed?

Christ the Ideal

We find in Jesus the perfect picture of gentleness and humility. As true God and true Man, He deserves adoration, worship, and praise. He became a human being for the purpose of redeeming us from our sins. He came to serve and to give His life as the ransom price demanded by the Law (see Mark 10:45). In John 10:11–18, we have a marvelous picture of this gentle Savior that is drawn by Jesus himself.

93. What does a shepherd do for his flock ordinarily?

94. If the shepherd lays down His life, won't the sheep be vulnerable to predators?

95. For whom does the Good Shepherd lay down His life?

96. Who killed Jesus?

97. What events does Jesus have in mind in verse 18? How are these the very heart and center of the Christian faith?

Lord God, Father Almighty, Maker of heaven and earth, great is Your mercy and goodness to men. You have made me and all creatures. Let Your Holy Spirit therefore work in me a grateful heart, that I may evermore thank and praise, serve and obey You, mindful of the fact that every good and perfect gift comes from You; in the name of Jesus. Amen.

Paul Bente (1886–1957)

Sing "The King of Love My Shepherd Is" (*LW* 412; *TLH* 431).

Words to Remember

The LORD is my shepherd; I shall not want. He makes me lie down in green pastures. He leads me beside still waters. He restores my soul. He leads me in paths of righteousness for his name's sake. Even though I walk through the valley of the shadow of death, I will fear no evil, for you are with me; your rod and your staff, they comfort me. You prepare a table before me in the presence of my enemies; you anoint my head with oil; my cup overflows. Surely goodness and mercy shall follow me all the days of my life, and I shall dwell in the house of the LORD forever. Psalm 23

To prepare for "Maintaining Self-Control," read Proverbs 25.

5

Maintaining Self-Control

What's in your wallet?

Commercial for Capital One

Anybody who has owned a credit card knows how difficult self-control can be sometimes. Our appetites and impulses often get the better of us and we find that we are our own worst enemies. We might embark on a self-improvement program and make good progress for a while. Sooner or later, however, we hit a plateau or get distracted by some other business in life and we end up right back where we started—or worse. At times we make decisions based on our desires only to find out later that our lack of self-control has created problems, sometimes serious problems, for us.

In Galatians 5:23, Paul lists "self-control" as one of the fruits of the Spirit, a gift of God that grows in the life of the Christian. He describes a life led by the Holy Spirit as one where the sinful nature "with its passions and desires" has been "crucified." The ability and strength to deny the self, to say no to our impulses and desires, comes from the Lord through faith in the One who died and rose for us. This sets up the daily struggle between the new person created by the Spirit at our Baptism and the old nature which wrestles with that new creation for control.

A Defenseless City

The term *self-control* occurs only once in most translations of the Old Testament, at Proverbs 25:28. There Solomon writes, "Like a city whose walls are broken down is a man who lacks self-control" (NIV).

98. What is the problem with a city whose walls are broken down?

99. How does this compare to a man without self-control?

100. What eventually will happen to both of them?

A Patient Man

On the other hand, the person who exercises self-control, generally speaking, has a much brighter future. Solomon writes in Proverbs 16:32, "Better a patient man than a warrior, a man who controls his temper than one who takes a city" (NIV).

101. Which man receives more fame and honor—the warrior who takes a city or the patient man who controls his temper?

102. Who accomplishes more in the end? Why?

103. Which is harder to do?

David and Saul

Twice in David's life we see this man of God exercise remarkable self-restraint. Samuel had anointed David to be king after rejecting Saul and his family (1 Samuel 15–16). David rose to prominence by defeating the giant, Goliath, who fought for the Philistines (chap. 17). Saul eventually became very jealous of David, even though David had become his son-in-law (chap. 18). Saul went so far as to try to kill David (chap. 19) and pursued him with the intent of ending his life. The Lord intervened when it looked like Saul might succeed (chap. 23).

Certainly David would have been justified in killing Saul when the opportunity presented itself, if for no other reason than self-defense. Read 1 Samuel 24 in order to answer the following questions.

Read verses 1–4.

104. How did the Lord deliver Saul into David's hands?

105. What did David do instead of killing Saul?

Read verses 5–7.
106. Why was David conscience-stricken?

107. Why does David let Saul go (see also 1 Samuel 26:9–11)?

Read verses 8–15.
108. How does David address Saul?

109. Why would it have been wrong to kill Saul?

110. In what way is David like a "dead dog" or a "flea"?

111. To whom does David turn for help and vindication?

Read verses 16–22.
112. How does Saul respond to David's speech?

113. What does Saul recognize about David?

114. What does Saul ask of David?

David and Bathsheba

If the previous story was a "close call," the account of David and Bathsheba is a "terrible fall" into sin due to a failure of godly self-restraint that led to adultery, murder, conspiracy, and family violence for generations. Read 2 Samuel 11:1–12:14 for the following answers.

Read 2 Samuel 11:1–5.

115. David was at home while his army was fighting in the field. Where should David have been?

116. At what point could this whole terrible episode have been avoided?

117. How do we know Bathsheba wasn't already pregnant when she slept with David?

Read verses 6–13.

118. How does David plan to cover up his adultery?

119. Why doesn't his plan work?

120. How does the loyalty of Uriah the Hittite contrast with David the king?

Read verses 14–24.
121. What is David's "plan B" for covering up his adultery?

122. Who else gets involved?

123. How does Joab modify David's plan to kill Uriah?

Read verses 25–27.
124. How does David's response reflect a disregard for the lives of the people that are fighting and dying for him?

125. At the end of chapter 11, it looks like David succeeded in covering up his sin. What was the Lord's opinion?

Confession and Absolution

God exposes David's sin by sending Nathan the prophet to David with a story.
Read 2 Samuel 12:1–9.
126. What story does Nathan tell David?

127. David seems more concerned over a lamb than the lives of his own men. What does he deserve for what he has done?

Read verses 10–14.
128. What three consequences will David and his family suffer as a result of his sin?

129. Does David receive forgiveness for his sin? Why?

Lord Jesus Christ, my Redeemer, You have given to Your dear church on earth and its faithful servants the sacred office of the keys. You invested this office with the promise that whatsoever they shall loose or bind on earth by these keys shall also be loosed or bound in heaven. I thank You, and eternally praise and glorify You, for Your gracious gift. Amen.

Johann Habermann (1516–90)

Sing "As Surely as I Live, God Said" (*LW* 235).

Words to Remember

For this very reason, make every effort to supplement your faith with virtue, and virtue with knowledge, and knowledge with self-control, and self-control with steadfastness, and steadfastness with godliness, and godliness with brotherly affection, and brotherly affection with love. For if these qualities are yours and are increasing, they keep you from being ineffective or unfruitful in the knowledge of our Lord Jesus Christ. 2 Peter 1:5–8

To prepare for "Valuing Self-Control," read James 3.

6

Valuing Self-Control

*Men are born with two eyes, but with one tongue, in order that
they should see twice as much as they say.*

Charles Caleb Colton

In our study of the Old Testament, we saw David fall into terrible
sin that only led to more sin and painful consequences because he did not
control his desire for Bathsheba.

Taming the Tongue

In the book of James, the author challenges us to control something
more difficult than temper or sexual desire—our tongue.

Read James 3:1–12.

130. What warning does he offer those who want to teach the faith
(vv. 1–2)? Why?

131. What point does James make with his analogy about horses
and ships (vv. 3–5)?

132. What commandment do we break when we call someone an
uncomplimentary name (see Matthew 5:21–22)? What penalty does God
exact for that sin?

133. Who invented lying (see John 8:44)?

134. Why is the tongue so difficult to control (v. 7)?

135. Can a Christian take God's name in vain or use foul language and still be a Christian (vv. 9–12)?

Run for the Prize

Read 1 Corinthians 9:24–27.

Paul offers us a positive model for understanding and applying self-control in our daily walk with Jesus. He invites us to compare our life on earth with an athlete's training, disciplining ourselves for the sake of the "prize" at the end.

136. What kind of "crown" do athletes strive to win?

137. How disciplined does an Olympic-class athlete have to be in order to win the gold medal?

138. Why should we practice self-control?

139. If we are saved by grace through faith in Jesus Christ alone, why bother to practice self-control?

Victory in the Wilderness

After John baptizes Jesus, the Holy Spirit leads Him into the wilderness to face severe temptation. The Father identified Jesus as His beloved Son with whom He is well pleased (Matthew 3:17). Satan puts that relationship to the test, much as Israel had been tested in the wilderness many centuries earlier. Anointed with the Holy Spirit (Matthew 3:16), Jesus faces Satan and shows us that godly self-control flows from a trust in the Father that relies on His Word alone. Read Matthew 4:1–11.

140. Normally people fasted during the day, eating before the sun rose and after it set. What point does Matthew make about the fast that Jesus endured prior to the first recorded temptation?

141. What would have been wrong with Jesus turning stones into bread?

142. What does Jesus use to fight Satan's temptations? Why?

143. Satan does not doubt that Jesus is the Son of God, yet he asks Jesus to put that relationship to the test by jumping off the temple wall in Jerusalem. Can you think of a time in your life when you have doubted the Lord's love for you and thought about testing Him to see if He cares?

144. People love power, wealth, and glory. Satan plays on that weakness in Jesus' final temptation. Yet at least two problems become apparent in his offer to Jesus about the kingdoms of the world. What are they?

145. What is Satan's ultimate goal in these temptations?

146. What additional information do Mark and Luke add when they record these events?

147. When does Jesus next hear the statement, "If you are the Son of God, then . . . "?

Christ the Ideal

Throughout the Gospels we read of the power and authority of Jesus Christ. True God and true man, He has the power to drive out evil spirits (Mark 1:21–28), even when thousands of them infest a person (5:1–20). He can cure the sick, even when all the doctors have failed (Luke 8:40–48). He even raised the dead (Mark 5:35–43)—even after they had begun to decay (John 11:38–44). Read the account of the crucifixion in any or all of the Gospels (Matthew 27:27–50; Mark 15:16–39; Luke 23:26–49; and John 19:1–30).

148. Did Jesus have the power to stop the crucifixion?

149. At what point could He have stopped it?

150. Why didn't He?

151. What kind of self-control would it take to endure all that He endured? Why did He endure it?

Dear Lord Jesus Christ, my longing is so great that I cannot express it in words. I know not how to ask. You see my heart. What more shall I say? My suffering is greater than my complaint can be. I cannot counsel myself with reasons nor comfort myself with my own courage. Comfortless, helpless, and forsaken, I am completely undone. My God, You will not abandon my hope. You will hear my prayer and satisfy my desires. My calling is to pray and await Your grace. It is Your calling to hear me and to fulfill my hope. Amen.

Martin Luther (1483–1546)

Sing "In the Cross of Christ I Glory" (*LW* 101; *TLH* 354).

Words to Remember

Create in me a clean heart, O God, and renew a right spirit within me. Cast me not away from your presence, and take not your Holy Spirit from me. Restore to me the joy of your salvation, and uphold me with a willing spirit. Psalm 51:10–12

Leader Guide

This guide is provided as a "safety net," a place to turn for help in answering questions and for enriching discussion. It will not answer every question raised in your class. Please read it, along with the questions, before class. Consult it in class only after exploring the Bible references and discussing what they teach. Please note the different abilities of your class members. Some will easily find the Bible passages listed in this study; others will struggle. To make participation easier, team up members of the class. For example, if a question asks you to look up several passages, assign one passage to one group, the second to another, and so on. Divide the work! Let participants present the answers they discover.

Some excellent hymns that may be sung at the opening of each session are "Almighty God, Your Word Is Cast" (*LW* 342; *TLH* 49), "Salvation unto Us Has Come" (*LW* 355; *TLH* 377), and "The Fruit of the Spirit" (*AGPS* 225).

1

Promised Faithfulness

Objectives

By the power of the Holy Spirit working through God's Word, participants will
- appreciate more fully the utter and complete reliability of God;
- see better the distinction and the connection between faith in God and faithful living for God;
- learn that faithfulness involves both confessing Christ and spreading the Gospel;
- find in Christ Jesus the perfect example of faithful living for the Father and the only real foundation for saving faith.

Opening

The session leader may want to spend time talking about the disappointments experienced by participants in their relationships. Without getting too personal, it may be possible to talk about times when parents or loved ones have let us down. Is God like that? The object of this lesson includes a resounding affirmation that "God is faithful!"

Abraham, a Study of God's Faithfulness

The story of Abram/Abraham covers Genesis 11:27–25:11. If participants have time, the leader may encourage them to read the entire section on their own. In this section, however, the class will look at only selected portions.

1. Note that God did not reveal to Abram the exact destination of his call. Abram responded faithfully, however, and headed towards Canaan (Palestine). The session leader might want to explain how much risk Abram assumed by leaving the town of Haran and the protection of

his extended family to go to a land where travelers were often "fair game" for all types of predators.

2. The seven parts of God's promise are identified in Genesis 12:2–3: (1) God will make Abraham into a great nation; (2) God will bless Abraham; (3) God will make Abraham's name great; (4) God will bless others and Abraham; (5) God will bless those who bless Abraham; (6) God will curse those who curse Abraham; and (7) God will bless all the nations of the earth through Abraham.

3. Genesis 12:4 describes Abram as seventy-five years old and childless at the time of the promise. The session leader may want to point out that the promise assumes children, both to make up the "great nation" of 12:2 and the final blessing of verse 3.

4. Abram points out that he has no children.

5. God tells Abram that his descendants will be more numerous than the stars in the sky.

6. God offers no proof. God's own faithfulness requires no proof.

7. Abram "believed the LORD, and He counted it to him as righteousness" (15:6). This verse plays a key role in Paul's theology (Romans 4) and for the writer of the epistle to the Hebrews (11:11–12). The session leader may want to direct the participants to look at the passage in Hebrews to see the emphasis the author places on God's faithfulness. Why does Abram believe? Because God gives him the faith to hold onto the promise in spite of all outward, physical circumstances.

8. God changes Abram's name from Abram ("Exalted Father") to Abraham ("Father of Many"). God stands ready to grant Abraham a child by Sarah (for her name change, see Genesis 17:15).

9. In 17:8, God adds the promise that He will give the land of Canaan to Abraham's descendants. The only piece of land that Abraham actually owned in his lifetime was his gravesite: the field of Machpelah (Genesis 23).

10. Circumcision served as a seal or affirmation of the covenant between God and Abraham. Remember that a covenant was "cut," that is, blood sealed the agreement.

11. God warns Abraham and his descendants to be faithful to His covenant. Faithlessness on the part of his descendants will lead to a loss of the land and a revocation of the covenant.

12. Abraham was one hundred years old at Isaac's birth.

13. Abraham waited twenty-five years for God to keep his promise.

Joshua, Faithful toward God

After many years of battle, God granted rest to the covenant people in the Promised Land. They had not finished their job of eradicating the inhabitants, and the Lord warned them about the dangers that lay ahead. Joshua wanted to remind the people of God's promises and His warnings and challenge them to fidelity in their lives—first to remain faithful to the Lord God alone and then also to obey the rest of the covenant. Read Joshua 23:14–16.

14. Joshua reminds the people that God is utterly faithful, having kept every single promise He made.

15. Just as God kept His promises, so they could be sure that He would follow through on His threats if they were to break the covenant and prove unfaithful.

16. The heart of the covenant between God and Israel appears in 23:16—worship the Lord God alone and serve Him only. This doesn't sound to modern ears like much of a problem, but the Israelites lived in a polytheistic society. Their neighbors worshiped false gods and the temptation would eventually prove to be too much. The first commandment ("You shall have no other gods before me," Exodus 20:3; Deuteronomy 5:7) serves as the fountainhead from which all the other commandments flow.

17. Joshua challenged the people to "fear the LORD." The session leader may want to explain that this includes saving faith as well as respect for God and the sinner's natural fear of His wrath. See Peter's use of this expression in Acts 10:34–35 as well.

18. Joshua boldly confessed his faith (Joshua 24:15). The session leader will want to make sure the participants don't imagine that we can choose God. He gives us faith through the Gospel and calls us to faithful living. Only someone who has faith in the one, true God can choose or not choose to serve Him.

19. Joshua warned them that God will not tolerate any syncretism. That is, He will not accept them if they worship other gods in addition to Him. He claims exclusive loyalty and fidelity on the part of His people.

20. Joshua's last command (24:14) reveals that the people still have "household gods" with them. Sadly, this blending of worship of the one, true God with false gods was common. Even Rachel, Jacob's wife, had stolen and hidden the "household gods" when they returned to Canaan (see Genesis 31:34).

The Messiah, Faithfulness Incarnate

The session leader can read Isaiah 52:13–53:12 to give class participants the picture that Isaiah paints of the coming Messiah: a perfect Servant of the Lord who suffers for the sins of the world. The leader will also want to talk about the fact that *faithfulness* is a relational term. It describes a relation to a person or standard. That is, you are faithful to someone or to something (like a code of ethics). This section asks the student to begin thinking about the will of God for the Messiah and His faithfulness in carrying that out.

21. The seven characteristics of the Spirit are listed in Isaiah 11:2–3: wisdom; understanding; counsel; might; knowledge; fear of the LORD; delight in the fear of the LORD. Remember that "fear of the LORD" involves a right relationship based on trust (see Psalm 130:4).

22. Participants may list the three characteristics in Isaiah 11:3–5: righteousness, equity, and faithfulness.

23. In verse 5, the prophet describes the Messiah as girded with righteousness and faithfulness. In context, *faithfulness*, clearly refers to fidelity towards God's will—ultimately, the cross. See also Isaiah 42:1–4. This the Messiah—Jesus Christ—did for us, earning forgiveness, life, and salvation.

2

Enduring Faithfulness

Objectives

By the power of the Holy Spirit working through God's Word, participants will

- appreciate more fully the utter and complete reliability of God;
- see better the distinction and the connection between faith in God and faithful living for God;
- learn that faithfulness involves both confessing Christ and spreading the Gospel;
- find in Christ Jesus the perfect example of faithful living for the Father and the only real foundation for saving faith.

Opening

The session leader may want to open the session with a voluntary discussion of the importance of faithfulness. Certainly, promises are broken and trust is abused, but how well could our society work without the faithfulness of elected officials? Doctors? Teachers? Electricians? Expand the discussion to include participants' expectations of others when it comes to the faithful performance of their duties.

God's Faithfulness

Because God keeps His promises, we can be certain of our salvation. Unlike people who swear eternal love for each other and six months later separate in bitterness, we can count on God. For Paul (and the other Scripture writers), God's faithfulness fully appears in Christ Jesus. Paul drives home this point in his letters to the Corinthians.

24. We find God's "Yes" exclusively in Christ Jesus. The session leader will want to take time to talk about salvation by grace through faith in Jesus alone (see Ephesians 2:8–9). Because salvation comes from

God without any contribution on our part, we can be absolutely certain of eternal life. If any good work on our part was required to gain salvation, no matter how small, God's "Yes" would have to be "Maybe" in Christ. "Maybe" you've done your good work well enough, "maybe" not. In such a case, no one could ever be sure of their salvation.

25. We can be certain of God's love because "while we were still sinners, Christ died for us" (Romans 5:8). The leader might use the following illustration. When we are dating, we put on our best clothes, look as nice as possible, and behave ourselves. We want to make a good impression so we don't drive the other person away. We certainly don't want that special someone to see us at our worst. Yet God knows us thoroughly as we are, sinners to the core, and still loves us in Christ Jesus. While we were at our worst, Christ died for us.

26. We stand firm in faith because God holds on to us. God gives us the gift of faith and with His strength we remain faithful throughout the hardest times of our lives. Not that we should grow complacent (1 Corinthians 10:1–13 will address that). Imagine the little child, hand in hand with its parent. It slips on ice but doesn't fall because the parent's strong hand holds on where the weak, small hand of the child could not. God, our heavenly Father, holds onto us like that.

27. The Father has given us His Holy Spirit as a deposit and seal of His faithfulness. When Judgment Day comes, we can be sure of acquittal because Jesus died and rose for us and His Holy Spirit dwells in us.

28. The Corinthians owe their gifts to God, who has faithfully provided every needed spiritual gift through the Gospel. They lack nothing they need for faith and faithful service to the Lord.

29. God will indeed keep us in saving faith to the end. 1 Thessalonians 5:23–24 concludes Paul's letter to that church with a prayer offering the same comfort and assurance.

Warning and Promise

30. Paul wants us to be confident in our salvation but not complacent. He warns us that we can always fall, no matter how secure we think we are (think of David and Bathsheba). He tells us in this Scripture that God's faithfulness does not give us an excuse to sin.

Paul's first point occurs in 1 Corinthians 10:12—don't take God's grace for granted. We can always fall.

31. Paul's second point appears in verse 13—everything that happens to us has happened to people in the past and God has proven faithful, always providing strength to bear it or a way out.

32. "God is faithful." He always keeps his promises and this serves as grounds for hope in time of testing and temptation (echoing the Old Testament theme in Deuteronomy 7:9).

Faithfulness under Pressure

In this section the participants will read a number of passages from Revelation to see that persecution tests and strengthens faithfulness.

33. The Christians in Smyrna must soon face intense persecution for "ten days," that is, for a short time.

34. We can measure faithfulness by what sacrifices it makes. In this case, "unto death." (See Mark 8:34–38; this introduces participants to the idea that the cross measures ultimate faithfulness.)

35. Jesus promises to give his faithful people the "crown of life," a victory wreath or crown signifying Christ's victory over sin, death, and the grave. The "second death" (eternal damnation) will not harm those who are faithful to Jesus even to the point of physical death.

36. Satan motivates all persecution of Christians. We want to remember that we fight against spiritual forces, not merely physical ones (see Ephesians 6:12).

37. Antipas confessed his faith in Jesus Christ, even under persecution, and paid the price for his faithfulness with his life.

38. Christians who live under hostile regimes should expect imprisonment and execution (Revelation 13:10).

39. Christ's people must endure patiently, remaining faithful to the Savior who died on the cross for us.

40. Revelation 14:12 makes the connection between faithfulness and Jesus explicit. We pray that we remain faithful to the person of Christ and to the Gospel and its truth.

In this short epistle John commends one man (Gaius) and warns another (Diotrephes) about their conduct in the church. Christian missionaries depended on the hospitality of fellow believers to advance the Gospel in the world. Traveling evangelists would find a place to stay, food to eat, and perhaps even a bit of financial support in a Christian home and community. Faithfulness includes providing this essential hospitality for the spreading of the Gospel in the world.

41. John writes to Gaius, a fellow believer.

42. For John, the "Truth" is both personal and propositional. Jesus is the Truth (John 1:14; 14:6) and the orthodox teaching about Him is also the truth. The session leader may refer the participants to 2 John 9–10 where John commands his readers to withhold hospitality from any who teach a false doctrine of Christ.

43. Gaius offered the brothers hospitality—lodging, food, and whatever else necessary.

Christ the Ideal

The author of Hebrews writes to Jewish Christians facing persecution for their faith. If they renounced Christ and returned to Judaism, they would be safe from persecution since Judaism was a licensed religion in the Roman Empire. However, salvation can be found only in Jesus Christ and the Gospel, far superior to Moses and the Law.

44. Jesus and Moses were both faithful to God, although the quality and degree of their fidelity varied greatly.

45. Moses failed to trust the Lord at Meribah, striking the rock twice instead of commanding the water to flow from it (Numbers 20:1–13). See also 1 Corinthians 10:3–4.

46. The people of God, joined by faith in Him, constitute God's house.

47. The faithfulness of Jesus is measured fully and finally at the cross. Setting aside His own welfare, He endured shame, agony, and damnation for us and paid the price for our entrance into the eternal Promised Land.

Hebrews 3 stressed the faithfulness of Jesus toward the Father. Hebrews 10 helps us understand that Jesus' faithfulness serves as the basis for our confidence of eternal life. We can count on Him who died and rose for us in that most critical of moments—when we stand in judgment before God's eternal throne.

48. We approach God only through Jesus, "with a true heart in full assurance of faith" (v. 22). The writer of Hebrews uses the temple and the curtain that separates the Holy of Holies to make his point. The session leader can take time to explain that our access to God in Christ Jesus far excels the access under Mosaic Law. There the high priest only could enter God's presence and then only once per year, on the Day of Atonement (Yom Kippur). Through faith in our High Priest, Jesus Christ, we have direct and immediate access to God at all times and in all places.

49. We can have a clear conscience before God because "the blood of His Son cleanses us from all sin" (1 John 1:7). The session leader may want to take this opportunity to talk about the blessings of Baptism and what the Holy Spirit accomplishes through this Sacrament (see Ephesians 5:25–27 and Titus 3:5–8 for similar imagery).

50. We hold onto the hope of eternal life with absolute confidence because "He who promised is faithful" (Hebrews 10:23). The faithfulness of God in Christ Jesus provides our eternal security.

51. The author encourages us in verse 25 to continue to meet together as God's people. God works faith and strength through the proclamation of His Word and the administration of His Sacraments, a marvelous focus on Christ, the faithful Son of God. Gathering together also provides an opportunity to encourage each other, both in the faith and in faithful living for the Lord who gave His life for us and rose for our justification.

3

Gentleness in Service

Objectives

By the power of the Holy Spirit working through God's Word, participants will
- see in Christ the gentle Good Shepherd who keeps his flock safe and sound;
- understand more clearly the gift of gentleness as an attitude that considers the welfare and needs of others ahead of the self;
- appreciate the compassion and caring that forms the foundation for gentleness as a way of life;
- connect gentleness with the unity of the Spirit and the bond of peace that we have in Christ Jesus.

Opening

As with the other fruits of the Spirit, gentleness does not come naturally. The world operates on competition, prizes aggressive behavior, and promotes self-interest. The session leader may want to ask participants how well gentle people fare in their world, whether at work or at school. What makes someone popular in school? What helps a career in the workplace?

The Hebrew word that often lies behind "gentle" or "gentleness" in the Old Testament may be translated "to be afflicted, to stoop down, to be humbled." Therefore Hebrew writers never use it to describe God, although David does praise God for "stooping down" to help him (2 Samuel 22:36). On the other hand, the Hebrew Scriptures do describe the coming Messiah (Christ) with this language. Especially in Isaiah, we see a picture of the Suffering Servant, perfectly faithful to God and yet severely afflicted for the sins of the world.

Isaiah's Words of Comfort

In chapter 40, Isaiah introduces us to the theme of forgiveness for a sinful and wayward people. God dealt mercifully with them by preserving a remnant and replanting them in Judah. He promises even greater blessing through the coming Messiah, the Suffering Servant who will redeem His people from their sin.

52. It may not be apparent yet, but God will pay the price for their sins Himself, in the Person of the Messiah, by taking the people's place under the Law and receiving their punishment in His Person (revealed most clearly in Isaiah 52:13–53:12 later in this session). A righteous God cannot merely turn a blind eye to sin; He must punish it.

53. John the Baptist fulfills the prophecy of Isaiah 40:3–4 (see Matthew 3:3; Mark 1:3; Luke 3:4; and John 1:23).

54. The messenger prepares the way by calling the people to repentance, a genuine confession of their sins, a heart-felt trust in God for grace and forgiveness, and a sincere desire to live according to God's will.

55. God reveals His glory primarily through the shame of the cross. He does the impossible—declares sinners righteous while retaining His own righteous integrity, all made possible by the incarnation, crucifixion, and resurrection of the Messiah.

56. Humanity and all its empires are no more than grass and flowers, which wither and die. The Word of the Lord endures forever and provides the only source of salvation and security (see also 1 Peter 1:24–25).

57. The two hallmarks of the Messiah's advent are power (Isaiah 40:10) and gentleness (v. 11). The session leader may want to take time to talk about the apparent contrast between these two characteristics and how they find perfect expression in Jesus, our Good Shepherd.

58. Isaiah opened this section with "comfort, comfort my people" and in verse 11 makes this comfort very vivid and personal. The session leader might consider opening the discussion at this point to allow participants to share those times when the Good Shepherd dealt gently and lovingly with them.

The Lord's Servant

59. The Servant is the Lord's Chosen One, anointed with the Spirit, commissioned to bring justice to the nations.

60. The Servant fulfills His commission in peace and gentleness (v. 2). The session leader may want to emphasize the fact that gentleness does not imply weakness. The Lord empowers the Servant with the Holy

Spirit; no one in the universe has more power and authority than this Servant-Messiah, yet He fulfills His mission with such gentleness that "a bruised reed He will not break, and a smoldering wick He will not snuff out."

Although the words "gentle" and "gentleness" do not appear in this text, the portrait of the Messiah that Isaiah paints offers us a tremendous picture of gentleness in the face of humiliation, suffering, and shameful death. Jesus understood this from the outset and at least three times during His public ministry predicted His crucifixion and resurrection.

61. God promises to raise up His Servant and highly exalt Him. The Servant will suffer for the sins of the world and give His life as a ransom for sinners, but God will vindicate Him in the end. The beginning and end of this Servant Song echo this wonderful promise.

62. The third Servant Song (Isaiah 50) answers this question. The Servant endures legal punishment (the beating) and shameful treatment (the pulling out of the beard) in obedience to the Lord's will and plan of salvation. The Gospels do not record a literal pulling out of Jesus' beard. The statement in Isaiah 50:6 may be taken as a figure of speech to describe extremely shameful and disrespectful treatment, suffered by Jesus at the hand of the mob, the soldiers, and His enemies.

63. Isaiah prophesies that the Messiah will be quite ordinary in appearance. This may help explain why his hometown people took such offense at Jesus' claim to be the Messiah (Christ) (see Matthew 13:53–58; Mark 6:1–6).

64. Isaiah 53:4–5 points specifically to the cross. We see this especially clearly in light of Deuteronomy 21:23. Originally Moses referred to the display of a dead body as proof of God's curse on that individual. By New Testament times, however, the passage was applied to those who suffered crucifixion (see Galatians 3:13–14 for Paul's application of this passage to Jesus' crucifixion).

65. By the cross, Jesus creates peace between God and humanity as well as peace between the divided peoples of the earth (see Paul's treatment of this theme in Ephesians 2). Mankind started the war against God in the Garden of Eden; Jesus wins the peace by laying down His life for all sinners at Golgotha.

66. Sheep are not intelligent animals. However, Isaiah does not insult us. He offers an honest and simple evaluation of God's people, comparing us to wandering sheep who desperately need the Good Shepherd.

67. The Servant shows perfect gentleness in accepting without complaint or violence the suffering, affliction, humiliation, and death God wills for Him. This actually comes very close to the classic Greek definition of the word we translate as "gentleness," that is, the noble acceptance of injustice and fate's cruel arrows. We might well think of Je-

sus' silence before Caiaphas (Matthew 26:63; Mark 14:61) and Pilate (John 19:8–9).

68. The perfect Servant suffers the law-breaker's fate because He substitutes Himself for sinners under the Law. God punishes the sins of the entire world in the Person of the Messiah (Christ).

69. Isaiah predicts that the Servant would be assigned a grave with the wicked but be actually buried with the wealthy, precisely what happened to Jesus (see Matthew 27:57–61; Mark 15:46; Luke 23:50–56; John 19:41). Ordinarily criminals would be buried in Potter's Field (if they were buried at all).

70. God elevates the Servant to the position of highest honor, raising Him from the dead and seating Him at His right hand.

71. We receive the forgiveness of sins as a result of His sacrifice—justification (God declares us without sin and having fulfilled His law) by grace through faith in this perfect Servant.

The Messiah King

The prophet Zechariah rebukes the people for dragging their feet on rebuilding the temple. A big part of their motivation for working on the temple is the advent of the messianic King pictured in these verses.

72. The people should rejoice because the King comes to bring them salvation and peace.

73. He comes humbly, riding on an ordinary beast of burden rather than a powerful and beautiful horse. He comes with gentleness for the purpose of laying down His life for their salvation. The session leader may want to point out that this passage points forward to the triumphal entry of Jesus at the beginning of Holy Week (Matthew 21:5; John 12:15).

74. The messianic King brings peace to the world and rules a kingdom that lasts forever. Through faith in Him, we are members of His kingdom.

4

Approaching Gentleness

Objectives

By the power of the Holy Spirit working through God's Word, participants will

- see in Christ the gentle Good Shepherd who keeps His flock safe and sound;
- understand more clearly the gift of gentleness as an attitude that considers the welfare and needs of others ahead of the self;
- appreciate the compassion and caring that forms the foundation for gentleness as a way of life;
- connect gentleness with the unity of the Spirit and the bond of peace that we have in Christ Jesus.

Opening

A gentle spirit, in contrast to aggressiveness or bullying, often wins the day. The session leader may want to begin this session by asking participants for examples of gentleness displayed to them—and the effects it had on their thinking, actions, and lives.

The Greek word behind "meek" in Matthew 5:5 is the same as the one Jesus uses to describe himself in Matthew 11:29 ("gentle" in NIV, ESV). The session leader can help participants understand that "meekness" or "gentleness" does not mean "weakness." Think of power and strength that reach out to others in love and tenderness and we begin to approach the idea that Jesus has in mind.

Peter's Advice

Peter addresses the case of the believing wife with an unbelieving husband. He advises the wife to fulfill her God-given role even in such trying circumstances. At the heart of his directives in these verses is a genuine trust in God to work through His Word as well as her non-verbal witness. The session leader can point out that nothing she does will "win" her husband for Christ. Only the Holy Spirit can do that. However, she serves as witness to Jesus Christ—as do all Christians.

75. A wife's non-verbal witness consists of her behavior. The session leader might take the opportunity to talk about the value of a verbal witness backed by action. Christians witness by their Gospel-produced behavior as well as their proclamation of the Gospel.

76. The world sees beauty in the externals—appearance, clothing, jewelry, and such.

77. God values inner beauty, particularly of a gentle and quiet spirit. Again, at the heart of such beauty is a simple faith in Jesus as Savior and Lord.

78. Peter's advice (like Paul's in Ephesians 5:22–25) may offend modern readers. However, they reflect God's design for marriage (Genesis 2) and were written under inspiration of the Holy Spirit. God's Word prevails over culture and serves as a much better guide.

Paul's Exhortation

Paul uses "gentle" and "gentleness" a number of times in his letters, often in the context of helping an erring fellow Christian. Gentleness flows from genuine concern for the brother or sister, a true love for the body of Christ and an appreciation of its unity in the Spirit.

79. Those who are spiritual (grown up in the faith) should deal gently with fellow Christians who are caught in a sin.

80. We carry each other's burden when we help each other deal with sin, error, and the whole range of life's problems we face.

81. Paul allows no room for a "holier than thou" attitude of pride and self-importance. We all stand as forgiven sinners before God, condemned by the Law and unable to save ourselves, but also forgiven by God's grace through Jesus Christ.

82. Perhaps Paul has in mind the law of love (John 13:35). Jesus calls us to love each other as he loves us (sacrificial, self-giving love measured at the cross).

83. We have been buried with Christ and raised with Him to a new life, including a new life-style (see Romans 6:1–11). In our Baptism, the Holy Spirit gave us a new birth and a new life, challenging us to live our faith on a daily basis.

84. Paul wants us to remain together, united outwardly in love as we are united inwardly by the Holy Spirit through faith in Jesus Christ.

The Corinthians provided an illustration of the opposite (1 Corinthians 3:1–3).

85. The "bond of peace" is the unity we have in Christ Jesus who has abolished the hostility between God and humanity as well as the dividing wall between people (see Ephesians 2).

86. We are to forgive as Christ has forgiven us. This is easy to say, hard to do, and possible only through the Spirit's work in our lives.

87. The love of Christ unites us. The session leader might remind participants of that hymn which begins "Blest be the tie that binds our hearts in Christian love."

The Yoke of Jesus

A *yoke* was a wooden or iron bar that went around the shoulders of an animal and attached to a plow or other instrument of work. It provides a vivid picture for the contrast between the way of the Law and the way of the Gospel in this section. The session leader might share with class participants the difficulty of keeping God's 623 (as they counted them) commandments even superficially. Read Matthew 11:25–30.

88. Entrance into the kingdom comes as a gift from Jesus, just like the Father's love for His children. Matthew 19:13–15 demonstrates this point. The rich young man of Matthew 19:16–26 goes away from Jesus very sad, even though he thinks he has kept the Law. The little children, having done nothing to earn Jesus' love, rejoice in His embrace as He blesses them.

89. In verse 27 Jesus professes to be the only way to the Father (as He makes explicit in John 14:6; see also Acts 4:12).

90. Jesus gives us rest from the impossible task of earning salvation under the Law.

91. His "yoke" is easy and His burden is light because He does all the work. Salvation comes as a free gift from Him who died and rose for us. Even faith, which receives the blessings of the cross, comes to us as a free gift.

92. Jesus' gentleness and humble heart are particularly evident as He welcomes sinners, battered by the world and condemned by the Law. He lays down His life for us to bring us the blessing of eternal life (see Matthew 5:1–12).

Christ the Ideal

The word *gentle* does not appear in this text, but the image of Jesus as our Good Shepherd speaks "gentleness" very clearly.

93. Ordinarily a shepherd guards the flock, pastures and waters it, and guides it to safety (see Psalm 23).

94. The shepherd that dies leaves his flock unprotected. Jesus, however, lays His life down only to pick it up again (see v. 18). Besides, in this case the sheep need the Shepherd to give His life for them.

95. Jesus gives His life as the ransom price for the whole world, Jews and Gentiles alike (v. 16).

96. We might say that the Jewish authorities killed Jesus or even that the Romans killed Him. We could even say that God put Him on the cross since that was the plan of salvation. However, Jesus makes the point that no one takes His life from Him. He gives it voluntarily. The session leader may want to note that crucifixion usually ended very quietly since death often came by asphyxiation and shock. Yet Jesus died with a loud voice, such an unusual way to die that it prompted the centurion in charge of the squad to say, "Surely this man was the Son of God" (Mark 15:39).

97. Jesus speaks in John 10:18 of His crucifixion on Good Friday and His resurrection on Easter Sunday. Jesus' sacrificial death and His glorious resurrection are central to the Church's proclamation and life, the very heart of Christianity.

5

Maintaining Self-Control

Objectives

By the power of the Holy Spirit working through God's Word, participants will
- appreciate the value of self-control in the daily practice of our faith;
- understand the conflict between our desires and passions on the one hand and the work of the Holy Spirit in our lives on the other;
- see the positive outcome of godly self-control and the terrible consequences of yielding to our desires;
- find in Christ Jesus, particularly in His suffering and death, the perfect model of obedient self-control empowered and motivated by love.

Opening

The session leader might open with an invitation to discuss the personal experiences that class participants have had exercising self-control. Depending on the size of the group and the level of comfort, many may express frustration at the difficulty in achieving goals set for themselves—credit cards, weight loss, smoking issues, exercise, and the like. The Christian often battles internally, the old sinful nature insisting on its selfish indulgences and the new creation in Christ Jesus striving to live a life pleasing to our heavenly Father. We do not face these struggles alone, however. The Holy Spirit works powerfully within our hearts and minds, using Word and Sacrament to bring forth the fruits of the Spirit listed by Paul in Galatians 5:22–23. The session leader should encourage participants in their daily war with the sinful nature because we fight these battles in the context of Christ's victory over sin, death, and Satan. Even when we lose, we have forgiveness through Him who loves us.

A Defenseless City

The word *self-control* occurs in the Old Testament only in Proverbs 25:28, where Solomon compares a defenseless city to a man who lacks the ability to control himself. The comparison would have been powerful to his original readers but may lack "punch" for the modern Bible student. Walls provided defense and protection for ancient cities, keeping foes at bay for years if necessary. They served also as a source of pride and confidence for the city's inhabitants.

98. A city with broken walls was vulnerable and exposed to every enemy, even to the wild animals at night.

99. Likewise, a person who lacks self-control exposes himself to disaster and shame whenever it comes his way.

100. Both will eventually come to ruin.

A Patient Man

Solomon offers a more positive comment in Proverbs 16:32. There he contrasts the famous warrior with the patient man who controls his temper.

101. The warrior receives great honor and fame, the adulation of his country, and the social position that goes with it. Most often no one notices the patient man who simply goes about his business.

102. Solomon helps us realize that the patient man frequently accomplishes much more in life than the warrior. The session leader might talk about the "flash in the pan" versus the "slow and steady" approach, like the old story about the turtle and the hare racing each other. The man who exercises self-control builds steadily throughout his life rather than accomplishing only one great thing.

103. Sometimes it is easier to do the "one great thing" than it is to hang in and make something out of life. We don't want to take anything away from the hero who does a great deed; yet it is true that much of the progress in the world and the benefits we enjoy in life come from people who patiently worked to improve our lives, controlling their temper and other emotions and desires.

David and Saul

The session leader will want to point out that God had selected Saul to be king. Samuel, the prophet of God, had anointed him (1 Samuel 10). Moses had foreseen this four hundred years earlier and had set up several rules for the king at that time. The session leader may want to have the class participants read Deuteronomy 17:14–20, where five requirements for the king are set forth. Only three kings ruled over a united Israel—Saul, David, and Solomon. After Solomon's death, Israel divided into two separate nations (the ten tribes of Israel or Ephraim to the north and the two tribes of Judah to the south). David understood that God had chosen Saul to be king and also understood that it was not his place to remove him.

104. God delivered Saul into David's hand by arranging it so that Saul went to relieve himself inside the cave where David and his men were hiding.

105. David secretly cut off a corner of Saul's robe while Saul was going to the bathroom.

106. David felt terrible pangs of conscience because he had dishonored Saul, perhaps by invading his privacy during a very private moment and certainly by cutting off a corner of his robe in secret.

107. David let Saul go because Saul was God's anointed, chosen king and because Saul was his father-in-law (there are Fourth Commandment issues here as well).

108. David calls Saul "My lord the king," "my master," "the LORD's anointed," and "my father."

109. David had not been commissioned by God to kill Saul—it would have been murder. David's self-control flows out of devotion to God and trust in Him to act according to His own will, even when David's life was on the line. This is a remarkable picture of faith in action.

110. David describes himself as a "dead dog" and a "flea" to emphasize the fact that he is no threat to Saul, as proven by the events in the cave.

111. David appeals to God for vindication and vows before the Lord that he will not harm Saul even though Saul is trying to kill him.

112. Saul responds with contrition and sorrow over his attempts to kill David. Unfortunately this is short-lived.

113. Saul recognizes that the Lord favors David and will hand over the kingdom of Israel to him instead of to Saul's own sons.

114. Saul asks David to spare his family when he becomes king. Ordinarily the first thing a new king would do upon assuming the throne is eliminate all members of the old dynasty. As readers of the Old Testament will see, David keeps his promise, another impressive display of self-control that flows out of trust in God and faithful loyalty to His will. The session leader may want to mention that David spared Saul's life on one other occasion as well (1 Samuel 26). He took Saul's spear and the water jug which lay by Saul's head while he was sleeping and refused to harm King Saul. David explains his reasons for not harming Saul in

1 Samuel 26:9–11, another expression of trust in the Lord and obedience to His will.

David and Bathsheba

The story of David and Bathsheba highlights the sad fact that a child of God can fall into the worst sins at any time, often through a simple lack of self-control. The session leader can share with the participants that David already had several wives. How simple it would have been for David, when he first saw Bathsheba, to turn around and walk away. Can the class participants look back on their lives and say the same thing?

115. David should have been with the army in the field. Why he stayed at the palace is not clear.

116. David could have avoided the whole mess by going with the army. The second occasion he could have avoided these terrible sins was when he first saw Bathsheba. All he needed was a little self-control at the right time.

117. The text notes that Bathsheba had just finished her time of ceremonial cleansing following her monthly menstrual cycle. She was not pregnant before sleeping with David.

118. David wants Uriah to sleep with his wife when he is on furlough.

119. David's plan fails because Uriah is loyal to the covenant.

120. Uriah, a foreigner, keeps covenant with the Lord and with his king. David, richly blessed by God and a member of God's covenant people by birth, has violated God's covenant and betrayed Uriah's loyalty.

121. David plans to have Uriah killed in battle.

122. David involves the general, Joab, in his conspiracy to commit murder.

123. Joab apparently doesn't want it to look suspicious that only Uriah dies in battle so he sends several soldiers to their death to hide the conspiracy. The session leader might ask the class participants what must have gone through these loyal soldiers' minds when they were ordered on this "suicide mission." Yet, faithful to their Lord, their king, and their general, they went.

124. David's response in 2 Samuel 11:25 seems calloused, almost cavalier. Contrast his concern for the lamb in 12:5–6.

125. The Lord was not pleased.

Confession and Absolution

126. Nathan tells the damning story of the poor man's lamb and the rich man's disregard.

127. David condemns himself in 12:5b, "the man who has done this deserves to die."

128. God outlines three consequences for David's sin: the sword will never depart from his house (intra-family violence and bloodshed); someone close to David (it turns out to be his son Absalom, 2 Samuel 16:21–22) will publicly sleep with his wives; and the child born to Bathsheba will die.

129. God forgives David for the sin after David has repented (2 Samuel 12:13) but he must still endure the consequences. Ultimately, God forgives David because Jesus Christ would die for his sins on the cross.

6

Valuing Self-Control

Objectives

By the power of the Holy Spirit working through God's Word, participants will

- affirm the importance of maintaining self-control when it comes to our speech;
- understand that the ultimate source of falsehood is our enemy, Satan;
- resolve to use the Lord's name only to bless, encourage, pray, praise, or give thanks;
- rejoice in Christ's victory over Satan through God's Word, especially as Christ is God's Word in human flesh;
- give thanks for Christ's death and resurrection, whereby we are assured of our forgiveness and eternal life;
- understand the conflict between our desires and passions on the one hand and the work of the Holy Spirit in our lives on the other;
- see the positive outcome of godly self-control and the terrible consequences of yielding to our desires;
- find in Christ Jesus, particularly in his suffering and death, the perfect model of obedient self-control empowered and motivated by love.

Opening

The session leader might open with an invitation to discuss the positive examples of self-control they have witnessed in others—especially in terms of speech. Contrast the "misplaced" word said at the inopportune time with a word not spoken or said later in gentleness. God our Father does not berate or belittle us, but rather speaks His condemning Word of Law followed by His restoring Word of Gospel. How might we do the same?

Taming the Tongue

James preaches self-control in our use of God's gift of language. We often don't think twice about gossiping, using God's name in vain, telling "little white lies," or using foul language.

130. James warns his readers that teachers of the faith (particularly including pastors) must be aware of the fact that they will be held strictly accountable for what they say. Since people (including teachers of the faith) stumble in life, including in their speech, a teacher (pastor) must be constantly in control of his tongue.

131. A small bit and bridle control a powerful horse. A tiny rudder steers a huge ship. Likewise, the tongue (which is relatively small) controls the entire body.

132. Matthew 5:21–22 records Jesus' condemnation of those who verbally abuse others. He tells us that God considers it a violation of the commandment "You shall not murder" and that it carries the (eternal) death penalty.

133. Satan invented lying, his native language (see John 8:44).

134. We find it nearly impossible to control our tongue because our speech reflects our nature—which is sinful. Because of sin we curse, swear, lie, deceive, gossip, and abuse others.

135. Using God's name in vain flows from unbelief and the influence of Satan. Christians undertake the daily challenge of drowning the old sinful nature under the sign of our Baptism, no easy task. Like rust on an automobile, verbal sin eats away at faith and the witness of the Christian to the world. If we use God's name in vain or use foul language, we confess our sins trusting that He forgives them through His Son, Jesus Christ.

Run for the Prize

Paul compares the Christian's life to an athlete's training. He does not want us to think that we earn our own salvation or that we contribute to it even a little bit through our own efforts. The session leader can help the participants understand that sin and faith don't mix well. Unrepentant sin eats away at faith and can eventually threaten our salvation. In this passage, the Holy Spirit challenges us to consider the value of strict self-control in the daily life of the child of God.

136. Greek has two words for "crown." One refers to the royal crown that kings wore (a "diadem"). The other denotes the garland or

wreath placed on the head of victorious athletes at the Olympic games. Paul refers to this type of crown in these verses, roughly equivalent to today's gold medal. Contrast the temporary life-span of the garland of greenery prized by athletes (and the fame that fades as quickly) with the eternal "prize" won for us by Jesus Christ.

137. An Olympic-class athlete subjects everything in life to the pursuit of the gold medal.

138. We should practice self-control for at least three reasons: (1) God wants us to do so; (2) it provides a better Christian witness; (3) a lack of self-control leads to disaster, sometimes even endangering our faith.

139. The session leader will want to emphasize that salvation comes entirely from God through faith in Jesus Christ. Even faith comes to us as a gift of the Holy Spirit through the means of grace (Ephesians 2:8–9). We want to practice self-control because we offer ourselves as "living sacrifice[s]" to God, who has given His Son as the sacrifice for our sin (see Romans 12).

Victory in the Wilderness

Adam and Eve faced the test of trust and self-control and failed (Genesis 3:1–6). Israel, God's son, faced a similar test in the wilderness and, like our original parents, failed. When Jesus faced temptation in the wilderness, He revealed what godly self-control looks like as He placed His trust entirely in the Father and accepted His will, even when it involved deprivation and suffering. The session leader might want to point out that the Greeks thought very highly of self-control as a virtue. They came at it from a very different perspective than Scripture, however. For them, self-control marked the person who lived the ideal life, independent and self-directed. In the Bible, self-control does not mean that a person chooses certain goals and attains them through necessary discipline. Rather, self-control refers to a firm and unwavering trust in God and the submission to His will necessary for holy living. Self-control comes to us as a gift of the Holy Spirit, developed and refined through trial, hardship, and temptation. Read Matthew 4:1–11.

140. Jesus fasted forty days and forty nights. Matthew wants his readers to grasp the severity of Jesus' hunger and the degree of self-control necessary for His success.

141. The issue is simple: do you trust God or not? As in the Garden of Eden and in the wilderness after the exodus, Satan works with food to drive a wedge between God and His child. The session leader might ask whether we can accept God's will in trust and faith if He wants us to have stones (hard times) rather than bread (comfort and ease).

142. Jesus uses the Word of God—Scripture—to fight Satan's temptations. The Bible is the only weapon we have. Paul calls it the "sword of the Spirit" (Ephesians 6:17) and the author of Hebrews says that it is "sharper than any two-edged sword" (Hebrews 4:12). The construction of the Greek conditional sentences ("If you are the Son of God, then . . .") indicates that Satan does not doubt Jesus' identity. Rather, he uses that Sonship to try to destroy the relationship of trust and obedience.

143. The session leader may want to start off by sharing a story about a time in life when doubt about God's love crept into the relationship we have with our loving Father. How did the situation turn out?

144. At least two major problems appear in the final temptation. First, worshiping Satan violates the First Commandment and destroys the relationship with God necessary for Sonship. Second, Satan has authority over this world only until Judgment Day. Like so many of his lies, partial truths hide the downside of the temptation. Until that final day, Satan is the prince of this world (John 12:31), the ruler of the age (Ephesians 2:2), prowling around like a hungry lion looking for lunch (1 Peter 5:8)—and we are on the menu!

145. Satan ultimately wants Jesus to fail in His journey to the cross. If Satan succeeds, no human being can receive salvation or enter heaven.

146. Marks tells us that Jesus was with the wild animals and that angels attended Him (Mark 1:13). Luke adds that Satan left Jesus "until an opportune time" (Luke 4:13, probably referring to the cross).

147. The next time we read "If you are the Son of God" is at the cross, Satan's final attempt to provoke Jesus to a loss of self-control and a failure in His mission to save us from our sins (Matthew 27:40; see v. 43 also; Luke 23:25).

The session leader will want to make the point that godly self-control has three identifiable components: (1) saving faith in the triune God; (2) submission to His will and agenda for us, not to our own goals and desires; (3) it is a gift of the Spirit, strengthened and empowered through Word and Sacrament.

Christ the Ideal

148. As God and man in one Person, Jesus definitely had the power to stop the crucifixion.

149. He could have stopped it at any time.

150. He didn't stop the proceedings because the Father willed it (the plan of salvation) and we absolutely needed it. Without His death on the cross under the Law in our place, we would face eternal damnation with no hope of salvation.

151. It is impossible to fathom the degree of self-control Jesus employed at His suffering and death. No mere human could have done it. Only Jesus could have done it. The session leader will want to emphasize the great truth that Jesus did it all out of love for us. In Christ's life, death, and resurrection we are assured of God's unfathomable—but by His grace believable—love for us.

Glossary

calling. See **vocation.**

covenant. A relationship or agreement not based on kinship. A contract. A "parity" covenant is an agreement between equals. A "suzerain" covenant is an agreement between a lord and his servant or between a strong nation and a weak nation.

double predestination. The false teaching that God eternally decreed who is to be saved and who is to be damned (with no hope of repentance).

election. From the Latin word that means "to choose." The biblical teaching that God chose believers through Christ to be His people and to inherit eternal life. God chose them purely by grace and not because of their good works or their faith.

fruit of the Spirit. Effects produced in believers by the indwelling of the Holy Spirit (Galatians 5:22–23). The good works produced by faith in Christ.

fear of the Lord. Reverence and trust in the Lord.

Gospel. The message of Christ's death and resurrection for the forgiveness of sins. The Holy Spirit works through the Gospel to create faith and convert people.

holistic. Applying to a whole subject. In theology, teaching that applies to a person as a whole instead of focusing solely on the spiritual or physical aspect of a person.

holy. Set apart for a divine purpose (e.g., Holy Scripture is set apart from all other types of writing). The Holy Spirit makes Christians holy (see **sanctification**).

justification. God declares sinners to be just, or righteous, for Christ's sake; that is, God has imputed or charged our sins to Christ, and He imputes or credits Christ's righteousness to us.

kinsman-redeemer. A person responsible for protecting vulnerable family members, especially in areas of inheritance.

Law. God's will that shows people how they should live (e.g., the Ten Commandments) and condemns their failure. The preaching of the Law is the cause of contrition.

parity. See **covenant.**

repentance. Sorrow for sin caused by the condemnation of the Law. Sometimes the word *repentance* is used in a broad way to describe all of conversion, including faith in God's mercy.

Sacrament. Literally, "something sacred." In the Lutheran Church a sacrament is a sacred act that (1) was instituted by God, (2) has a visible element, and (3) offers the forgiveness of sins earned by Christ. The sacraments include Baptism, the Lord's Supper, and Absolution (if one counts the pastor as the visible element; see Apology XII, 41; XIII, 3–5; Large Catechism IV, 74).

sanctification. The spiritual growth that follows justification by grace through faith in Christ.

Semitic. From the Hebrew name *Shem*, who was an ancestor of the Jewish people and other Middle Eastern groups (Genesis 10:1, 21–31). A word used to distinguish the descendants of Shem and their culture (e.g., Hebrew is a *Semitic* language).

suzerain. See **covenant.**

theology of glory. The idea that the true knowledge of God comes from the study of nature, which reflects God's glory. Also, the belief that suffering should not be part of the Christian life because God's people always triumph.

vocation. From the Latin word for *calling*. A person's occupation or duties before God. For example, a person may serve as a father, a husband, and an engineer. Each calling comes with different responsibilities.